The Travels of Ben Sira

STANLEY NELSON

Books by Stanley Nelson

POETRY

The Passion of Tammuz — Bellosguardo Press (1959)
Idlewild — The Smith, 1970 (first printing)
1971 (second printing)
The Brooklyn Book of the Dead — The Smith (1971)
Chirico Eyes — Midnight Sun Press (1976)

THEATRE

The Scene/1 (editor, with Harry Smith) — New Egypt/Horizon
(1972)
The Scene/2 (editor) — The Smith/New Egypt (1974)
The Scene/3 (editor) — The Smith/New Egypt (1976)
The Scene/4 (editor) — The Smith/New Egypt (1977)

FICTION

The Unknowable Light of the Alien (Stories)
— Seagull Publications (Spring 1978)

The Travels
of Ben Sira

STANLEY NELSON

THE SMITH
by arrangement with Horizon Press
New York ✖ 1978

For My Daughters
Celia and Lycette

The [legend], voicing the prevalent belief in the possibility of impregnation without physical contact, relates that the daughter of the prophet Jeremiah entered a hot bath soon after her father had left it, and there received her father's seed. The son of this unusual conception was named Ben Zera, "son of seed," but when he grew older and came to understand the significance of his name he was ashamed of it and changed it to Ben Sira, by which pseudonym we know him as the author of *Ecclesiasticus*.
Jewish Magic and Superstition, Joshua Trachtenberg, Behrman's Jewish Book House, New York (1939).

That which has been is now;
and that which is to be hath already been;
and God requireth that which is past.
Ecclesiastes, 3:15

morning: December 24
morning: December 25

Winter   Dawn   and from the height of the buildings

muted whiteness. Selah.   Rest
is what I seek
                    Rest
                            for the traveller. Prophet

of many lands, many rivers
                                    and voices. Here

I have come at last
among the winter
                        crowd whose breath
                        exudes the fragrance of eluctable

Tombs. On you
                    friends, passersby

may depend my accomplishments
this day of our
                        day of our
                        day of
                        our Lord, *this* day

In the year.... Recall me, I insist

My disguise: briefcase,
London tweeds, camel hair coat, tyrolean hat
Italian shoes

                    incredibly polished. It is necessary

to emerge
                    this morning   *this*   morning   before

                    this once-holiest of
                                    Days

9

as all Christian gentlemen emerge—though I am
Unchristian
                and dress no differently on other days—

to make my way
across the bridge
                into the City. In many
Cities
        you have known me
        in my disguise
                        as I moved with prophet's robe
and staff
            through Memphis and Abydos, Ur and Damascus
            Alexandria and Troy. Blind, perhaps, as the Greek
                oracle

or humble as the 36 wisemen
                            of the hassids
                                        you have seen
                                            me
and turned your head
and not noticed—not even
                        in your mirror—and I have gone
                        my way in the wintry   the dawn

of winter.

But never, perhaps,
have I passed so humbly

As in this land   this northern land   where my shadow is
        white
against the snow
                    and I appear as one of you
and you do not ask
What it is that beats
                    under my breast. *Almighty*

10

God, give us grace
that we may cast away

the work of darkness

and put upon us
the armor of light   the night

                              is nearly over
                              the day has almost dawned

there will be signs in the sun and moon and stars
and on the earth there will be dismay among the nations
and bewilderment at the roar of the surging sea

And Mattathias and his sons tore open their clothes
and put on sackcloth and grieved bitterly. And Mattathias

          and his sons   now in this time

of this mortal life   *in which thy son*

                                        As I approach
the bridge
          this bridge

                    hallowed

                                        in song

                                        and set foot
on its ramp

                    WATCHTOWER/*the golden tablets*
                         gleam   in the sun
                                        clutching my briefcase
(that might contain, who knows, an apocalyptic scroll)

I have become
          Anonymous

                                    an ancient river
                                              Idol   winter
Dream ungarlanded with winter
                                        Sleep. There, on either side
the works of men
                        assault me, smokestacks
                                        and turrets, glass
                                        edges close me in
                                        with shadow, o
                                        miracle sanctified
By everyman
this December

solstice   this
                        consecrated morning I am moving
Up the ramp
                        into rapturous funnels that lead to hulking
gothic-
                arched supports
                                hulking in my path

                                like wingéd Assyrian bulls

                                I am among

the choiring strings
                                of cables   *the works* of man   Harp
                                        urging toward
Heaven
                but downward- inclining
                                        the Liberty   the Liberty

wind whipping my legs
                                        must keep in
Shape
                pierced
                                the blood   by a crest of bridges

12

                              Ships
veering out where the river broadens
becoming bay and
                Ocean
                        in the great breast of a harbor
                        Turneresque

                                        TIRE
CHANGING ON BRIDGE
                Roadways

                    I am moving
            ever upward, one part of me

leaving off my flesh
                    or, as the master said, my
Earthly garment
                    and still another part far
from the core, but the part
you see, o passerby,
                    wrapping round my

robes, pulling my tyrolean hat, buttoning
the collar of my camel's hair
coat
        smell: is it garbage
                        or the sea
gulping frost and wind
                    I hardly see
the various birds
                    escaped from a harbor
                    light
                        on water   how lovely
peaceful
            ripples
                Have I seen cherubs

                            on the golden dome?

                                                13

PHOTOGRAPHS   PERMITTED
FIRST BANK
            OF
    CITY

CHUCK/SUB

                              Steps   where did they
Steps
            descend   descend   the subway   I cannot
Emerge
            the
                  Subway
                        breeding-place
of nettles and saltflats
                  why
                        the exit
through subway
            NO FUME

but I come up a Plaza/a Square/a Park   Snow

            Ancestral   Epochal
                        Anonymous   forms
                            in the sky

    Snow in my
                  little Park   I will
sit

            be late

                  Fuck it

14

Sit POLICE-
LINE DO NOT CROSS

Personages

Person who the

hell *Christ* *mas* *Christ* *mas*
mas *mas* Papal
Persona in my little

Park where I saw juncos
move along move along *Let us go*
and make a treaty
with the heathen around us
under the trees of winter
Stands/the High Priest
robes and mitre stolen
from Mattathias' time

(police on horse-
back/old-
fashioned)

Office/go

Stairs up THREE FLIGHTS *must keep*
in shape hi boss WHAT'S NEW
late *so* *what?* cruddy black crumbling
Steps BULBS BULBS *explode in my*
brain flourescent flakes of the INSANE

Financial Chronicle

SERVING THE FINANCIAL
AND BUSINESS COMMUNITY
Community

Peter and Paul   the loaves   the disciples
Mattathias and his sons   The Early Christians   Wandering

                                        Saints
Stacks of releases
                    You will edit   You will choose
and hand releases
                to writers
                            who will give you back releases
                                                    to edit

Gideon, we will soon move
to new offices
in a building where escalators glide
and the air is continually
humidified
and the windows do not open

                        Gideon, the publisher
calls me,
            but my name is   not the part you see, o passersby

Airway, Inc.

—SECURITIES REGISTERED—

The company, 333 Butternut Drive,
Dewitt, N.Y., filed a registration
statement with SEC on Dec. 15 $12,000
of 7 per cent subordinated debentures
$4,000,000 of 6½ per cent 3,000
shares of membership common

The Community
    the brotherhood of stocks and bonds   o gnosis of eco-
nomic stratification   Pythagorean mysteries of CORPORATE/
                        MUNICIPAL FINANCING

16

via Thomson & McKinnon Auchincloss Inc.
                                        Snow
the bridges   the epochs
                              I shiver
beggars in the park
                        huddle on benches
                        for warmth, under

                        the winter trees   Maybe a magi
among them
              a wiseacre
                        Wiseman   Techtonics
of archaic archons
                        Gideon, he calls me
but my name is

              Irenaeus/Ben Sira/Paul
              Ieou and Melshesidek

are powers behind or symbolized by
BANKING LOAN-AND-DEPOSIT RATIOS
the sun and moon   Falconbridge Nickel   With
and Without Euro $ *And Jesus and his disciples*
soar aloft   Qualidex Fund/Allright Auto   5-YEAR CALL
PROTECTION RATED BAA BY MOODY'S   *into the aerial regions*
via Hornblower & Weeks Hemphill, Noyes
the WAY OF THE MIDST   they have accordingly
been bound by Icou in the Fate-Shere   accordingly
bonded by taxable totals to be publicly offered   O-T-C
Market Acme Visible under Adamas Three Hundred and Sixty
of this Brood All this refers to IRI Property Units
Registered as Sons of the Pleroma Bid Michigan
Pipeline Winkleman Stores Inc. President of Abacus
said the statement by Mr. Goldfine saying Abacus
offered relevant derogatory information
Who is also in these Extracts
represented as the Chief Questioner desires to be informed
as to why the aerial Ways of the Midst

ARE MONEY SUPPLY MEASUREMENTS TO BE TRUSTED
AS A MONETARY POLICY GUIDE OR 'FRIEDMANITE' DE-
TERMINANT LET ALONE AS AN INDICATOR OF ECO-
NOMIC ACTIVITY??

                                        Yet there is also
for Friedmanite or Ophite
                        a ting of Otherness   even here
in this office
                where thick, faded glass

                you cannot see through
Reflects
        flourescence   ancient river
                                Idol   Encompassed
by inner bulbs we Transcend *what is*
                                and our own Natures
Otherotherworldly
                white snow bare   trees yellow
faded newspapers bound in red
                                tomes   *I am where*
the river broadens
                becoming bay and Ocean   Even here
becomes
                as cubicular secretaries adjust their glasses
                                        one whole
Hopper scene/uhoh
                black girl with big boobs
                                        bursts
                                        my Pleroma
hardon
        in my Pleroma
                        phone jingleslices
                                        my Pleroma
                                        Hello
Sophie
        my barren

18

                Wifie of 30 years   *I will go into that region
with my consort*   Yes, your list, hello

Bulbs
Tinsel
Cord
But
        I'm not even Christian   Yes/will do   Goodbye

Sophie the Barren
                pondering Aeons wailing
                your songs of repentance

of suffering and repentance   I have spoken to you
                in many cycles   o passerby
of the First Mystery
                prior to Unorder   but you ignore
me and Sophie
        shivering   in a Winter Wonder
                land of the barren earth

and you hear the outeronly
                unto chronicled financials   NASDAQS
        NASDAQS
                NASDAQS/"the above letters represent
"National Association of Security Dealers Automated
        Quotation System"
                        Ben Sira
                        it is time you travelled
far
        What profit hath man
        of all his labor

                I spoke with my own heart, saying:
I am going out to lunch

                    Yes, Gideon, go out
                              and look at new offices
Cold   numb   Woosh   wind   bright

Sun
      noon-hour   legs   Walk   walkfast   keep
in
      Shape   for   all event   ual   ities
Un
      Shaping
                  fast/past
                              Trinity Church
Three   Thrice   Christ/Father/Holy

Christ   but Jung says
                        Four   Holy
Tetragrammaton
                        the roll of Jung
                                    ian   Yangs
me

      gold-tipped   gothic spires   *again*
the gothic spires
                  "last chance to get your tiny Santa
Clause" says man on corner
and little Clauses tremble
round my feet
                  lunch crowds
                              Hey Lady
Watch
        my coat-sleeves
        pigeons may fly out   you are brushing against my

                                    Christ
                                          it's cold go
get
      lunch   Soup   Yep that's for

20

me   Jiffy Food
                Shop/revolve
                        through doors
I revolve, cycle to cycle
Maybe a wizened
Wiseman
Maybe a chronicler
of commerce, 36
In each generation   I am never noticed
I eat at wooden counters
My feet may be bleeding
In my Italian shoes
Snow blotched
In the passages   of these vast cities
      I am confronted   at midday

                   SEXUAL POLITICS

girl next to me at counter
flicks pages in my face/come on with your
Emancipation
You stupid
           lesbian chick Ah   my soup
I slurp as men in booths
            "brothers are afraid
they will be euchred out of their corporation"

               but it's *Christ, the brothers*
afraid of
    liquidating
        Oh Christ not
        here too
        gulp
        down coffee   pay get out
Fast

light in the park and the gothic
Arch   crest of bridges   my

Ascension
        can't go back to
Releases; me, a scholar

                        of gnostic tomes   I will walk
as icons assault me

I have solsticean time   Marylaps and babes   up lower Bway
almost pleasant
                these streets of warehouses and winter
                air gashed with excelsior

        oh little streets of Ole Bway

FASHION NOOK YANKEL HOUSE PILE
FABRICS NOAM HAT CORP. NOVELTY
GALPERIN BROS.
                bros.   *bros.*   Strange

hassidic Jews
                unload handtrucks, shake
their frosty earlocks this day
before Christmas

                In the days of Hasmoneans,
Mattathias, son of Johannes, the High Priest, and his sons
When the iniquitous powers of Greece rose up   And thereupon
The children announced to the oracle of Thy House
cleansed Thy temple, purified Thy Sanctuary, kindled lights
in Thy holy courts, and appointed these eight days of Hanukkah
to give thanks and praise

miraculous

the candles burned for eight days
without oil

candleabra (menorah)

I am interested   I was in
                    my Pleroma
                                        pierced
by freaky
            far-out hippy fuckups
                                        they are congregating at the
Intersection
            huddled in blankets muttering
            tarot/ching
                        of astrologic forms   hearyatalkinto
Me, Ezekiel
            you are the white bird
            resuming its monotonous flight   "Starting

with the indisputable fact
that man's life and happiness
are largely dependent upon phenomena
in the heavens, that the fertility
of the soil is dependent upon the sun shining in the heavens,
as well as upon the rain that comes from heaven,
it was a natural step for the priests to prefer a theory
of complete accord

between phenomena observed in the heaven
and occurences on earth"

                        On Earth/occurs

a gigantic wooden cube   under the winter sun
            of lower Manhattan   Anonymous logo
of hippiedom   futuristic cube   round which nekkids run
      Babelian   And the House which Solomon
built for the Lord   three score cubits, and the breadth thereof
      for the House was built of stone made ready at the quarry
and there was neither hammer nor axe nor any tool of iron
      heard in the House   And in the Sanctuary
he made two cherubim of olive-wood, each ten cubits
            High   and you, Ben Sira

                              must pass through the shadow

of this Cube
                  to stop
                        for coffee
                              Some
                                    Wanderer/Me

'There is nothing better for man
than to eat and drink'
                        so I will get me
a tuna and rye
                  and a cup of coffee
                  BUN 'N BURG
I will rest
                  and stare at hippies
                  Brueghling in the snow
near NEDICKS   WOOLWORTH   Skip

the tuna, just a cup of java, please
                              that's no good bread
                              for me
Ah drink it down, Gideon,
                        and get your fatass moving
                        into the frosty light

24

is

Soph

ie

left you to wander among Friedmanite crowds
whose breath

gives off the fragrance
of Exportable Fuels/New

Issues

I am moving, Sophie,

ever into this winter day
ascending with the Sonship

leaving off attributes

mithraic
carrying a Son
huddled
against my breast
though
my feet
may be bleeding, his garments
are in the briefcase I think
I am holding

Uptown

I move

Thus

Holderlin   is   to   Grace   Heidegger   Church   Calvary
Ohgod

not confronted

by   The

Church

again gargoylean

gothiCalvary

the pagan norse

land   *whose*   land   *this*
land is my
land this land is your
land

a little spire of trees
and ivy in the churchyard   o tannenbaum
o tiny
                plastic figures   in the manger   Santa
baby Santa
             baby   Spikes of the Church   assault my eyes

moveonmoveon
            you don't belong here
                                    Jew
                            huddle in your
winterclothes and
            justkeepwalkin'

            but
            in my mind's eye I always see
the stone, bowed
            figures of Authority   Strange

transneighborhood of antique stores and mystic bookshops
my feet yearn for
            STOP ITCH IN SECONDS
            Binal Cream

                        desert sands/warm kingdoms

ACHOO   *God*
                bless you
merry gentleman
Let nothing you
                Dismay

                        nothingmedismayoubetcha
                        transducted to terminal 14th
                        Street   14th Street   mecca of
Shlock

26

but at least you are *somewhere*   Yessir   BUY
NOW FOR XMAS
AND SAVE
A SMALL
DEPOSIT
WILL HOLD
ANY ITEM
UNTIL WANTED
USE OUR
LAYAWAY

PLAN   *Museum of Media*

            S. KLEIN   ANNEX NEXT DOOR

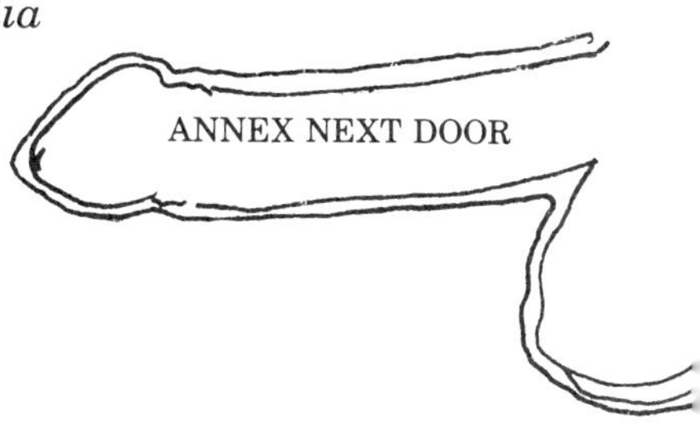

Wow
        phallic-like

                    Use   Use   Plan

Salvation
        Army Salvation
                Army, black-uniformed, brassed
                and accordioned

                with red-banded hats   sal-
                                        vation me o
                                        I hear you

(talkin')   His name shall be called Wonderful Counsellor,
                The MightyGod, The Everlasting Father
                        The Prince of Peace   *Why*
do bells of christmas ring?
Why do little children sing?

                              I dunno. but I go past you
                    heathen-goyim, to
                    rest in another

                                        park where no-one is but
ragamuffins snitching smokes
                    I blink   I breathe   I am alone
sudden in the park
                    snow is lightly falling   little
Chinks
          on the footpaths   and what's this a squirrel
so help me
                              he doesn't mind the snow at all
          maybe I should stay in this little
park forever
                    frozen   everyone has gone away
but a lithe
                    transvestite lugging Christmas packages
he/*she*?
          looks back at me I'm
          almost tempted   what's it like
          with a transvestite   No

You must go, Gideon
to the great city of
Ninevah
                    toward those cute little
                    Spanish girls and nuns
                    standing under white plastic
                              umbrellas

                    you must find new offices even
the pigeons have abandoned this park
and the squirrels hide under benches

                              move Uptown

                                                  in

Dread

                              we are in suspense

                                              Or, to put

      it more precisely
                    dread holds

us in suspense   because it makes what-is-in totality

              slip away   from   us

                          Hence
we

      too   as existents in the

              midst of what-is   slip

                          away from   our

                                              selves

                                              along

                          with it.   for

                                                  this
                        reason it is not
you or *I*
                    that has the uncanny feeling/but

                                        one
            in the

              trepidation

                   of this
                         suspense
                                    wherethere

                         is nothing
                                    to hold onto
                                    pure

              Da-sein

                                              Remains

                                              so too

Ben Sira continues his journey
midst
              shadow and sundials and clock-
                                              leaning things

l'Anabastic

anaßase

look up look up see the
towers and zag
                    through ziggurats

         NAT BLATT   CLOTHES

              and I have come to the Great Department Store
Nirvana
                    Alleloo
                              willgo
                              in   will go in
past big Santa standing
                         near fake brick
chimneys

                    buy bagels   Bagels!   Bagels!   *Baggele*
Oyoyoy
          Heywatch
                              you again lesbian
lady goshoveyour
                    sexual politics   through

revolving doors
                    always revolving doors

                    I wish you a Merry

Christmas   JESUS
      OF NAZARETH, KING OF THE JEWS

King
          Rehaboamjeraboamasabaasanadabelohomrije
          hosophatahaziahje
          horamjehoahzpekaheza
          kiah   Elijah

the Tishbite/Pre
                    cursor

          The Circumcision of Christ/*Christ*

how mucky
          Every newly-confirmed
          member of the Church
          is recommended
          to make some preparation of the mind and spirit
          before attending Holy
          Communion   Communion   *I recommend*

          THE NATIVITY OF OUR LORD
                    or
          THE BIRTHDAY OF CHRIST

                        commonly called
                        Christmas Day
                        (December 25)   *of the mind*
                                                         and spirit

some preparation
                    Any
                        preparation   O   Lord   Jesus

                                    only-
                                        begotten
                                                of married
Virgin
        /all creation
                        through him/none
                                    without him/in
him   life and light   the light still shines the darkness
            has never put it
                        out/Thou

hath loved righteousness and hated iniquity
Therefore God, thy God, hath anointed thee

                                        Darkness pierced
                                    with thy blood
                                            and the sun became
Blood
            and hail and fireand
                        B1   And there appeared

a great wonder in heaven
a woman clothed with
the sun and the moon under
her feet
and upon her head a crown
of twelve stars

                                   And the woman was called
Sophie   Barreness of
                         EternoLitsphere   fell   from light
into the muckdarkblooded
Mystery
                 and called that light
Lion-faced
                 psalmed a mourning
             regioned air searching for a

                                         Son, her
                                               Son, wake
up Gideon, wherethehellyabeen
the time is verypast
                         to wanderfar in Herodsville   very
                                               verypast
                 noonhour/lunchhour
a nip in the air unlike
                 Anyother
                         lookatyour

                         Breath   fragrance
of Winter
         eluctable
                 Tombs   *And he shall rise up*
                              at the voice of a bird

Financial   Chronicle   serving the   Financial
             and Business Community   You   Ben Sira
WandererMe   willedit
                         releases   handoutandwriteandedit
         Releases
                 white sheets of snow
                 floating out the window

                                   on City Hall

33

> †Inertial Motors Corp.
> †Delta Mobile Homes, Inc.
> †American Option Writers Income Fund, Inc.
> †Peg Leg Bates Country Club, Inc.
> †Ingram Manufacturing Co.

Inc., Inc.,
        adinka
            Finance economist
            is OPTIMISTIC about the money

market outlook in APPLAUDING
                        the President's blunt frontal
attack on domestic and international theologies   *theologies*
I yearn

tosearchamongthewayandfind
                        ofsoulandspirit
                        and so I came
among the winter crowd

                        and rested, disguised,
                        on a bench on the Bridge
                        and the cars zoomed by
                        under my rump
                        and GAIR
                        GAIR INDUSTRIAL BUILDINGS

O Stonehenge
voiceof

        the Celtic Crosses   barbarians   barbarians
crossing the Northern seas

                    into
my Heartland

34

                    with fierce nostrils, their graveyard
Crosses

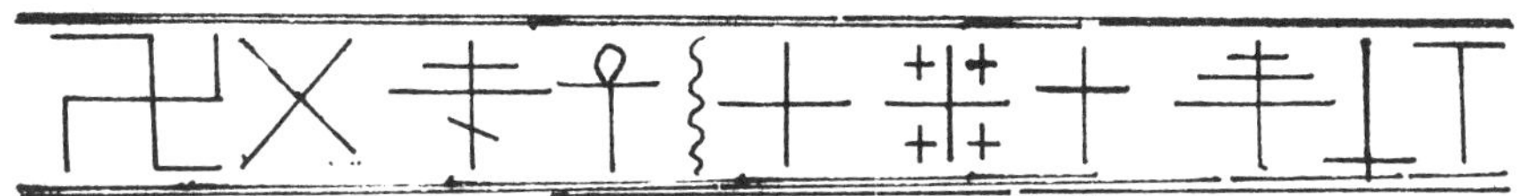

                    no medit   no medit
terranean

            Me

            the ancient writers regarded as homogeneous
            all the fair-haired peoples dwelling north of the Alps
            the Greeks terming them all
            KELTOI

                        And Ben Sira saw

under the winter sun
at the foot of the City
on lower Bway

        that the barbarians had builded them a wooden
        Cube   giganticfuturistic   and he witnessed further that

        young long-haired ones
                        Assembled

                                    under the Cube

            with their wives and husbands and children and lovers
And he saw further that
                        they builded them fires
                        and huddled together for warmth
And often performed rituals

of strangeness
singing indelicate harsh-throated songs
accompanying themselves on instruments

plucked, blown or thudded
with utmost screechiness of which Ben Sira
hadneverseenthelike

And Mattathias
and his friends mustered a force and struck down
sinners in their anger and in their wrath
the heathen and the alien and those who disobeyed
the Law and they went about and tore down the false altars
and forcibly circumcised all the uncircumcised children
and they drove the arrogant before them   So the work
prospered in their hands

And the time
veryfar   verypast   drew near

for Mattathias
to die
to die

Shipwreck
Existenz   Transcendence
of other
ness
Dread reveals

Nothing

Dread

strikes us
dumb
because what-is-in totality

36

                         slips
                                  away
and thus forces Nothing to the fore

                                             all
                       affirmation

                       fails in
                       the face
                                 of it. The

                                  fact
that
        when
                  we
                       are
                            caught

              in the uncanniness of dread

                                        we often try
                            to break

the empty silence with words spoken
at random
                  only
                       proves
                                 the presence

                                        of Nothing   Or
As the preacher said:
                  Drink water from your own cistern
                       And fresh water from your own well
                  Lest your springs overflow in public
                       Like rivulets in the open streets

no
  rivuletshere

            only congealed
                          Ice   Brr   like Ezekiel's
Heaven
        a shadowon
                  the snow   unrecognized

                                in my disguise   I long to
leave off
          attributes, all
          fleshly garments

                          movingeverupward
                  floating
                  among the breezy spheres/rings
        of the seforith

            what's this?   hardon

      In my pleroma
                  jinglesliced again
                                in my pleroma
                my pleroma
                      shattered
                            bulbs in my brain
compromised unsaintly by salty
                            Flesh
                            unfortunate
                  bulge beneath my camel's hair coat
        somehow mind has grasped

bigboobed   blackassed   officebitch

        Return   Return

                        of the Wanderer   too   tired

so horny   so tired   mustget

        Secondwind   exercise   everyday

go to
        massageparlor like big Exec/ get
                                jerkoff job
go to
        pornoshop on forty-second
flip through
                brown packet of bareass
go to
        fuckfilm   sitwithbig
                      hardon

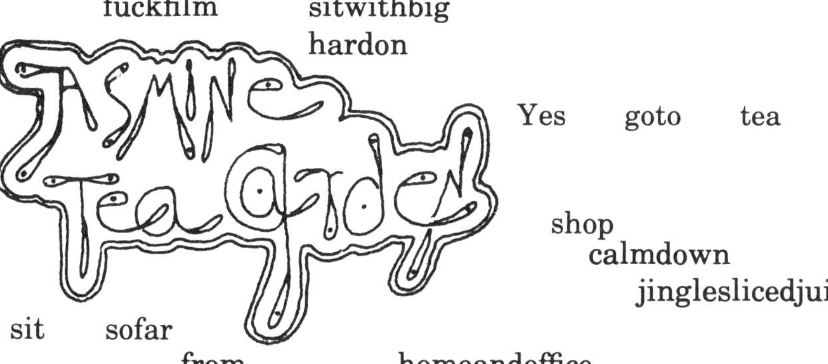

                                      Yes   goto   tea

                                shop
                                    calmdown
                                        jingleslicedjuices
sit   sofar
            from   homeandoffice

                                      Warmth
in steamy cups
openup
sinuses

            what's   thislady   againshove   I
hadthatseat   now   lassietwat
            nomoreroom
                            twittingme
                    SEXUAL
                            POLITICS

wait   seat   rush
    sit   shrimp   chicken   pork
                Fried Rice

                            Fried Rice
                                    Fried Rice
Lo
    Mein Chow
                Mein
little dainty-fingered ladies
lifting dainty cups
                        greentea
WOW
                one spears my ankle
                        with her heel so
                dainty

    aah   Warmth   formebringing
        Wonton Soup for Wanton
                                Man   horror
flick TV
            fatassed
            lady shoves her thighs

                            slow-thighed
                            Monster in the Desert
against mine
                Well
that feels good

                rough beast   rough beast   what
slouches

        Yankele Yeats Johnny
                            Donne   Yeah that
                        sagood
                                Momma

it is pleasant and good
to sit on this winter after
noon watching snowy steam
on Chinese teashop windows

surrounded by soft thighs
and warmsmells
for I am myself somewhat
pacificly passive
with extra epidermal tissue

Jungsuc

      cubus

         shadesof

            Tiresius

               feeling sortof

Gushy

     if I had a handkerchief
     I'd cry

          delicate
       serve the Chinese chicks
         with grace and

Fidelity

       their minds I Chinged
       by quietus

         and musicspheres   the action
of wood has reference

        to the upper trigram

      which is the symbol both   Sun

              of wind

   and wood.   from wood boats
and ships

are made
           on which the great stream may be
      Crossed.
           Crossed. For we are all
in some way or other

           kept asunder by our secrets   instead of
      seeking

           through confession
           to bridge the abyss that separates us
      from one another

           we choose the easy byway of deceptive openness
and illusion.   In saying this   So

           Renunciation   Self-Sacrifice   is not a gesture
      of greatness
                to be praised and copied   L(l)ove

aloneshares   it
                alone
                          can commune, but
      renunciation and self-sacrifice

                are the ways
                          the ways
                          of isolation and illusion

Thou
who didst come into this world
knowing in advance, from the first moment
                          of thy life that thy death
                          was our redemption

Death   Redemption

                        but the delicate-fingered
yellow-skinned
              waitress
                        appears with the check   parousia
again I am hoisted
                        through revolving
              Doors
                        Verti
                              go
              are   you
running with me

                  Jesus   Am I moving with
The Man
              of End-time
                        scoring with the Ancient
cloud-rider

        of Days

                  sashaying through the Universe
        with the testament of forms
                                          easily
as moisture through air

                        or
am I moving
              on Herald Square
              Square/Square
                        Herald
LOOK BEFORE YOU CROSS (ON THE CORNER OF COURSE)

park of granite benches
                        methuslaed with noise
                        tickertaped with scraps of

The Times/Daily
          News since the *Herald* and the *Sun* and the *World-*
                    Telegram went propitiously

                                        out of business

soleavethispark
it belongs to the pigeons
it is not
          my little park
          of Snow
where I saw Juncos   or the park of the manger
                    and the little Christchild
and the nuns with plastic umbrellas
                              Then
he began to denounce
the cities where most of his work had been done,
because they did not repent: 'Woe to you, Chorazin, woe to you
Bethsada!' Woe
to them that are at ease in Zion
And to them that are secure in the mountains
of Samaria
                              Jerusalem
was uninhabited like a wilderness
                              Joy
vanished from Jacob
                    And the flute and harp ceased to play
                    And Judas and his brother went forth
and made war on the sons of Esau in the country to the south
MenorahMenorahMenor

                                        to
                                   JAMES

GORDEN BENNETT
               (1795-1872)
               FOUNDER OF THE NEW YORK HERALD
               AND TO HIS SON
               JAMES GORDON BENNET (1848-1872)

Through   Whose   Vision   Enterprise   Herald
     World's   Great   News   paper

The Bronze Figures of Minerva and the Bell Ringers are the
work of Anton Jean Carlos. They stood from 1895 to 1921
Above the Cornice of James Gordon Bennett's New York
Herald Tribune at the North Side of Herald Square
and
Tolled the active hours to the millions

                                        God

whoever looks at these Ozymandiac
plaques and memorials
plunked in the middle of Herald Square
                                   the works of man
                              assault me
                                              Funds
for the restoration
              were provided by subscription of
              business organizations
                         bus. organizations bus.
                         Organizations
O Christ

              "brothers are afraid
                         they will be euchred out of their
                                        corporations"

what
              bus.
                         orgs   Peg

Leg Bates Option Income
Writers Delta Home Fund
                         Ingram via McKinnon via Auchin
     closs
                                                        45

                    via   via

                                              Hark
the bells
             at fadingafternoon
             summoningBen
Siras
        now another bellringer calls
        a bearded Bway Santa
                        moving now among the hordes the
             dollies and handtrucks and dressracks
        and between the columns of the Greenwich Savings Bank
                             fake little lighted Christmas
trees   Yea
                   Darkness   and not light   Shallnot
the day of the Lord be
                        Darkness   and   notlight
             Even verydark
                        and nobright
                                     ness?

"I can't believe it; this woman used to teach me math"

"So he took some cold cuts"

"He aint never had a good ass, that's for sure"

"I used to crochet when I was in college"

"Santa lives in Finland"
                              BINYL
CREAM   Ass
                           itch   Stop
sinuses aching
             allover
                        pain
cold

46

Brr
        colder
                coldest inside
                all my pleroma
    though now a warm drizzle slushes the snow
and the day grows gray and
                                gloomy
                                    suit baggy, crotch
Sweating   fleshfleshing
                needashave
                                Un
                                    kempt "Say
buddy, can you tell me where's 1407?"   *Shut up*
Spic   Noshouldnasaidthat
Liberalme
            but must look chic, snappy, executivy   look for
drycleaning ticket   *wherethehellwhich*   *pocket*   Aah
    gotit   gotit   Sophie   you can't
nag me
        Old Lady
                        sits on steampipe   Aeons and
Multitides pass
                and Christmas carols
                blare from CHOCK FULL O' NUTS
                Kindness
                            Adds Sweetness to
Everything
            Kind Words Are The Music
                of the World
                                Produce Happiness, Cost
                Us Nothing

                        Now I turn up my collar
and peering through the cafeteria window
                                    see man shlurping
                                                hot
tea with lemon and stale   blueberry muffin

the host   *the wine*

again a cold sun
above the buildings
                    Iron
                        Signum of the waning year

in the
        sky   in the sky
                            o taste the light and blood
                      they are warring
the light and darkness
                      in Manichean splendor   On this day
                            it is ordained

who shall live and who shall die
who shall attain the measure of man's days
who shall perish by fire and who by water
who by sword and who by beast
who by hunger and who by thirst
who by earthquake and who by plague
who by strangling and who by stoning
who shall have rest and who shall go wandering
who shall be tranquil and who shall be distant
who shall be at ease and who shall be afflicted
who shall be brought low and who shall be exalted

**BUT REPENTENCE PRAYER AND RIGHTEOUSNESS
AVERT THE SEVERE DECREE**

DECREE
          decree   *Mygod*   I feel it
alright, the
          de   cre   e   eee   And Herod
decreed

          And Mattathias and Judas Macca   beus   theyall

48

when Jesus was born in
Bethlehem of Judea in the days Of Herod the King
behold   from the east to Jerusalem   Saying
where is he   where is he   that is born
            King of the Jews?
              Then Herod was exceeding wroth   wanting to slay
the little children   all that were born in Bethlehem   And

Moses said unto Pharaoh
And

all of the firstborn in the land of Egypt shall die
from the firstborn of Pharaoh that sitteth on the throne, even
unto
the firstborn of the handmaiden that sitteth behind the mill   So

        May my heart be to me in the House of hearts
        my heart be to me in the House of hearts
        may be to my heart, may it rest in me
        or I shall not eat of the cakes of Osiris
        on the side east of the Lake of Flowers   *a boat   in*
                                        thy going down
                                        and in thy sailing up

    Pharaonic

            I am marching along
Bway pharaoh
                splendored in Akhnaton robes
                                                O Atonsun
o hymnals
            gongs
                        at my innards
                        and clock-
leaning things
                    shattered
                            bulbs in my brain
                                    flakes

                                        of the insane

a flame-stove
constant in the night, warmth
of Proustian tea and snow-flurries

                              I forgot on the dry hot
                                        sands of

Mesopotamia
                  as I moved with prophet's robe
                  through Memphis and Abydos, Ur
                  and Damascus
                  Alexandria and Troy   Marseilles and London
                                                      and Ulan
            Bator   dry wind
                                           of Mesopotami
ansun
                  dials

                        Meso   messin   mess

of noise, rock, rubble
fenderscamper
                  Subway crowds   noexit   plenty FUME
drillspiercespine
                        ears shake with blastout

must crap   holditin   Crap   holdit   pay

toilet
            no change   fortitude
                                    cocoons the Stoic   alkalizes

Syrupy bowels

            Vavooooooooomm   that northern wind
                  knocks my knees, rives my throat   and my feet
must be bleeding

50

under my sexy
Continental shoes now incredibly

Unpolished

and the flesh
windsdown, fleshall is
hardons and throbbing
by Nature and cycles
                        pierceable   but the spiritsoul
ghostholian
                dovebaptized   yearns to break free rebellious
clapping and shouting   its own Fulleristic
                            synchronies
                            groping its own enchiridians

IN ADAM'S FIRST SIN, MANY KINDS
OF SIN WERE INVOLVED

O Christ,
        it is hard to find the way
        among this wintercrowd

though my palms come together and pray
and my head is bowed
                        o passerby
you do not notice me
moving with riversmells and skyflashes
winter dream
            ungarlanded with winter sleep   GO
TO CHURCH
            READ BIBLE
            JESUS SAVES YOU
            SPIRIT IN FLESH CARES

oul
atisfaction

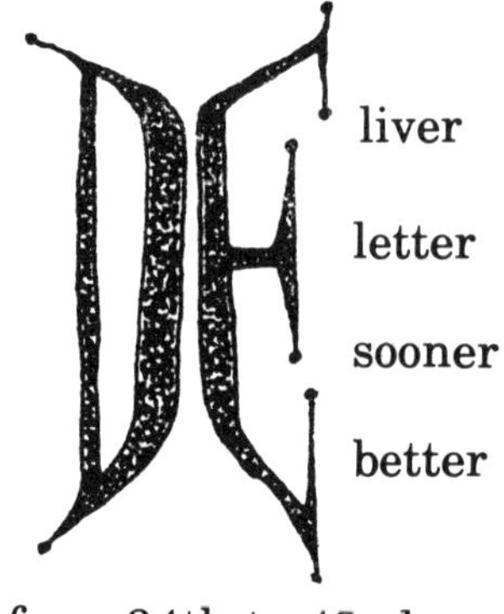

liver

letter

sooner

better

              fast   trip

              fasttrip

from 34th to 42nd   42nd   really shuttled
overhere
        Man
           took your own A
                train, Midnight
             SeeSee

                Ridered   to Porno

Country
       COUPLES   SEE   *SINGLES*
           ADULT MOVIES
       RELAX—PRIVATE BATHS
(*what* do you do
       in your private baths?)
           And the time has come

Ben Sira
     to browse through pornoship

          There is no assuaging of thy hurt
          The wound is grievous
or as the preacher sayeth:
        A time to embrace and a time
        to refrain from embracing

Meaning:

Everyman the Wanderer
must pause now and deal with

                     hisfleshall   hardonsandthrobbing
thronal
       holyplace   Altarmuch
Assaulted
        midst afternoon excelsior/Adeste

Fideles
     EXCITING PAPERBACKS   Thick
and Throbbing
          Sticky Pants   Shove It
             plus
          8 mmm
        Film
         MAGAZINES
          and
         Rubber Novelties
         ADULTS ONLY
       You Must be 21

                      mags
   INTERSEX/INCLOSE   The Sexhibitionists   Hard

Rider Joyful and Making
It Triumphant Star Light Star
Bright Lap Up O Come Ye
Lust The Sexually Unsatisfied
Male Bottoms Are Tops Fall
On Your Knees Sado-Rape Swap
Master Lost House
Wife Pictorial
Manual of Secondary Positions Three Wise
Men in Merrie
       Scotland

                        BLIMPIE
                        BYNIL
                        Doll House
                        Massage Parlor   All
                             Types Massage by Lovely Female
                                                      Models

getout   getoutfast
                         cantstand   these furtive redfaced men

homoparlor
                 homoparlor
                             must look like that myself

do I have it
               now the ultimate hardon
               lacking
               lassietwat and female companionship
I'll never see Sophie
                    again
                    The passions are separated from Sophia
and she remains as the substance of the highest of
the lower planes   and this material, man, is
                                     an inn or dwelling-place

but where   o where   do I relieve this
               bulgeache   eternal
                                             Adamic sin
                 black bitch   wriggles on
                                             8th Ave pimp
lurks in doorway
                 aach   howmessy
                                             Bessie
          get off street
                      trip   too heavy
                 Man
                                     heavy

54

can't go bulging beserk on
                           8th Ave   willgo   will
goto
            fuckfilm   Yes   Continuous
               11   a.   m.   11
p.   m.
              AdamsEves   in   Nudewet
Marathon
          bowheaded   collarup   shamefacedly
     furtive   wallet fumble   drop
                       change   fall on

        knees
             pickup   pay   *pay* five smackeroos too
sneering cashier
        slink to seat
        oh   shit   lights on   lights
                turn off   can't
be   seen
        darknow music   ready   cozyVoyeur
pacificly
passive
     in the darkness   roll'em

    That Great Technicolor Hardon In The Sky

man kisscs
mons

IT IS PROBABLE THAT CHILDREN ARE
INVOLVED IN THE GUILT NOT ONLY OF THE
FIRST PAIR, BUT OF THEIR OWN
IMMEDIATE PARENTS

*Let his left hand be under my head
And his right hand embrace me*

tongue lurks at *My beloved put his hand at the hold of the door*
clitoris   *And my heart was moved for him*

IT IS DIFFICULT TO DECIDE
WHETHER THE SINS OF A MAN'S
OTHER PROGENITORS ARE
IMPUTED TO HIM

man licks clitoral
juices sucks at
shaft

cuntstuff in man's
cheek, woman arches, coming,
thighs quiver, twatlips
heave

THE GUILT OF THE FIRST SIN IS SO
GREAT THAT IT CAN BE WASHED AWAY
ONLY IN THE BLOOD OF THE MEDIATOR,
JESUS CHRIST

Skilltongue swirls
goes guildy on
undershaft, twaddles
scrotum
womanmouth
suctionshlurps penis

bulge, womanhand
grabsroot
backsquats
shoves it

CHRIST WAS NOT

    mustgo   mustgo
       can't
           gowith   penisbulge

I rose up to open to my beloved   let

your fingers do the walking

                                        Ex   *plo*   *sion*

                        REGENERATED IN THE BAPTISM
                        OF JOHN, BUT SUBMITTED TO
                        IT TO GIVE US AN EXAMPLE OF HUMILITY,
                        JUST AS HE SUBMITTED TO DEATH, NOT AS
                        THE PUNISHMENT OF SIN, BUT TO TAKE
                        AWAY THE SIN OF THE WORLD

sinofthe   sinof
                                        take   took   taken
Never
            happened
                        Never   Ever
Woooshed
            mybrain   Dreamed
                        bulbs   aburst
flakes
            leaving off   gaveitup   gaveitup   fleshall
unthrobbed
            burnt sacrifice   odor of Isaac
            risen to the Almighty's
                                        Nostrils   All

Attributes
There was when naught
Was; nay even that naught
Was not aught of things that are

And Ben Sira came at Duskfall to the great Plaza
and gazed in awe at the great Evergreen of Christ
And pondered the Lipschitzean Statue that supports the World

Feeling the weight of Titusarch and Templesynagogues
Kneeling in his heart before the Archangels of the Promenade
In their white Robes flowing, blowing Ram's Horn Trumpets

> *St. Patrick's bell*
> *St. Patrick's bell*
> *(Hail the babe Emmanuel)*
> *Tolls the hour between Heaven and Hell.*

And Ben Sira walked in the shadow of the Public Crucifix
Unnoticed by Worshippers on Holiday, ancient River Idol,
Anonymous, blue-lidded, shadowless. And he alone,
Ben Sira, saw the White Birds across the Sky
Resume their monotonous Flights, the Sun
    engulfed by the River,
Glow of the Rose-Ascending House and the Preincarnate
    Signet Ring,
Each door doomed
By the Blood of the Lamb.

> *How regally the spires*
> *Hang suspended from the fires;*
> *Eternal is the glass*
> *Where magic of the saints is cast;*
> *And through the iron spheres of sound*
> *Forms are dropping to the ground;*
> *Angels running through the streets*
> *On whispering holy feet.*

Whispering   someone

        cuddlesnear

                whisperbreathes   in my

                                Ear

ineluctable breathof
                wiseacre
                        angel
                Maybe
ruddycheeked with
                Joy
                        he that receiveth
                        the seed in stony places
and he that receiveth the seed
among the thorns
                        in this time   be ye alway

            Ready
                        Always see
                stone, bowed figures of
                                Authority
                                and still I feel
the weight of synagogues, weight
                                of the centuries
                                weight of the
                                        Cross of the
Bloodguilt
            JesusFather, I have sinned
            and I have caused others
                                to sin
                                still I feel
                                    that desert Voice
in my ribs like branching fire

PROMETHEUS

59

TEACHER IN EVERY ART
BROUGHT THE FIRE THAT HAS PROVED
TO MORTALS A MEANS TO MIGHTY
ENDS   do I alone   Ben Sire/Iraneus/Melchisedek
                    among the wintercrowd
          hear the pierce
     of the Ramshorn?

Lovers, children on the artificial ice, red-parkaed woolen
Scarfed

               pilgrims with polaroids
               become a scene from Brueghel or
                                   Norman Rockwell
     Sun
          is bruegheled too
                         in it last throes blackening
with River,
          Flags of all nations in the wind are
bowing, bowing to
                    Christ   ye shall hear of
                    Wars
                         and rumors of
          War
                    At icelevel
Sweepers glide by at evening
their brushes and skates
have the sound of grinding
                         weary shoppers sprawl on benches
                         thankful for sprigs of evergreen
                         resting for the final preparations
          of mind and spirit
               some preparation
                              is   re   quired

We ourselves

confirm
that dread reveals   Nothing

when

we have
got
over our dread
in

the
lucid

vision
which supervenes while yet the experience

is

fresh
in our
memory
we must needs
say that what we were afraid
of actually

Nothing
Night
Night   sudden the crowds
by troth
have disappeared
I am alone
in the great Plaza
where will I go?
where will I go?
this land
myland   Norseland
Thor
land   paganwind

rives and knocks
                    the year's
                                        Declension
                         swirling
                                             the snow
                                   against glass buildings
                    The period
in which the German people
retained some vivid recollection
of their common origin
                                   remains beyond our knowledge;
                                   we know nothing
                                   definite about this bygone age

The original abyss, say the bards, stretched from the land
of ice, darkness and mist in the north to the land of fire
in the south. Rivers came from the south and flowed
toward the land of ice; there they became frostbound
and died in the icy vastness
                                   land   of ice; frost

                                        and eternal
Silence
             and I came
                         out of the land of fire
Go
             to Temple, Ben Sira
                                        it is the Feast of Lights
                                                  and you are
Hasmonean and Maccabee
                                   but the synagoguedoors
                                   are locked are locked
the windows are dark
                                   Silence
                                             only the crunch
                    of newspaper trucks

62

                                        buses speeding to the
Terminal
                    laying off for
                                        Christmas Eve   God
            How I miss the nut-flavored wine
                                                    Chants
                of my forbears
                                        the sound of dradles
smell of wax
at the simple lighting of

                                        Menorah
                            and the warm yearning arms of
Sophie
            but I am moving
                                everupward   leaving off, I
                                                have left off this
Attribute
            offleshall
                            hardons and throbbing   *Quickly*
                            O Light, vindicate
                                                and avenge me
I have travelled
                    veryfar   verypast
                                                        NASDAQ
Thomas & McKinnon
                        Auchincloss Inc.
                                                at last
I have come
                to the gothic-spired
                                        Cathedral
On this Eve of Eves
            Wanderer
                        Me
                                    Anonymous
            I am moving with the silent crowd becoming

            Worshipper

                              leaving off my
                        camelshair and Italian shoes
                                              where
                                        is my briefcase?
barefoot in monkrobes
                                  my breath has become
the incense
                    of medieval
                                        Wintersday
O Fathers
                    I hear your gregorian
                                              Voices
Irenaeus
                  Ori
                            gen
                                        John Chrysos
        tom
                    Augustine   Duns
                                                    Scotus
Cyril and
                    Nestorius   St. Thomas
                                                    Aquinas
                  Valens of Mursa
                                        and Basel
                                                    of Ancyra
                        deep woodwind
                                              paracletish names
like doves descending
                                        Christfather   Holy
Spirit
            Open
                        my heart's Iconasta
                                              to your
                    Entrance
                                        of what
or when
            is the supreme Godhead
        composed?

is it

the three hypostases of

Father, Son and

Holy Spirit

or is the latter

at the summit

of an angelic order?
where
is the Unconquered Sun?   can

God and man

form a single nature

(physis)

of which the divine

Word

is active

subject?   who

will fight the Pneumotachi?   And see

Cathedraldoors

are open

beckoning

Love

that

creates

us

Love

that

saves

us

Love

that

en

velops

us

                              It is warm here surrounded
                              by strange Latin
                                            Places   trans
ept
        nave
                   sacrest
                              y   clerestor

                              y
                                     *Agnus Dei, qui tollis peccata
                                     mundi*
                                            :misere nobis

                   and you too, Ben Sira
        chanted
                     celibate
                              ly   cenobitic
     in roughhewn
                              chapels   your life
     resonant
                     a wooden flute   comingling
        incense
                     and breath on a winter's
                                            day   matins
     and lauds
                     terces and high
                                     masses   nocturnes
     and vespers
                              anthems and   litanies   pre
     faces
                     prayers with seven
                                            psalms

             Compliances
                                     framework
        of a timetable

66

                              I am at
        the baptismal font   drops of blood are on
            my forehead
                                  taste of flesh
                                          in my mouth

with water and repentance
but he that cometh after me
is mightier than I
                                    he shall baptize you
                                    with the Holy Ghost
                                    and with fire
the people who sat in darkness
saw a great light   and to those
who sat in the region and shadow
                                        of death   light

        is sprung up   the night
    is nearly over   the day
                                    has almost dawned
          signs
                      in the sun and moon and stars
          dismay   bewilderment
    among the nations   at the roar of the surging sea
                                            look   hear

        I am approaching   The Baldachin
                          the voices
        of the MainAltar
                          eternal   are thy mercies,
    Lord
              in the Old
                          Testament   God

               promised the
                              Redeemer
                                        the fleche
                  rises to gothic arches
                                        my ascension

                                        this December
solstice   this
                              consecrated morning I am moving
            into rapturous funnels
                                        Altar
of St. Anthony
                                        Altar
of St. John
                                        Altar
of St. Stanislaus Kosta
                                        Altar
of St. Michael and St. Louis

                  and Brigid and Bernard and Theresa
         of the Infant
                  Jesus   and the Holy

            Family
                  O Christ
                              within
            myself
                  I have come
                              to your altar

            Silhouette
                         postured   supplicant
                                                         al
            a whole burnt
                              offering   *behold the fire*
                                          and wood

but where

        is the lamb?

              here I am

Jesus,

    the ram in the thicket

                bound

  for sacrifice

    let the guilt   of centuries

               well up

flow from me

    like white

         Incense   for truly

I have drunk

    the bloodwine

        and feasted on thy flesh

leaving off

    the attributes

      of many lands and rivers

  nakedshivering

    leaving off

        even the attributes of

    Everyman

      O Christ

        Forgive   Forgive

give a sign

    a drop

      of blood   thy smell

is in my nostrils

    thy taste

        thick on my tongue   all

all

  is cleansed in thy fire   I am

verycold

       my scars

             verygreat   my wound

throbs

            leav

    ing

      I

        inner

                          I

FAINT

       heaven to heaven   beyondall

         increate

     my own

         pleroma

    sleep

        long   dawnlight

           through stainedglass windows

                     Voices

Winter   Ben Sira   wakes and moves

everunto
outer
                    ness

                                        Sun

Dawn

                                comingles with the

                                                morningstar

                                                        Amen

                        Amen

                                Selah

The First Vision: Ben Sira in the Great Department Store

And Ben Sira dreamed of a Great Department Store
where forests grow out of elves' ears, the elves reclining
on WHITE SPRAY SNOW

And Ben Sira dreamed of a Great Department Store
where elevators never stop ascending on mystic rungs

    where the glass jars contain secret formulae
of berries and menses and the left eye of a hoopoe   of
Little Nothing Sheer Panty Hose Isotonic Gloves for
Hands Beautiful by Arie   Personalized

    Christmas Stockings   And Ben Sira dreamed of a
      Great Department Store where eternal chandeliers
glisten overhead and rivulets flow in the dark basements
or salesgirls with halos in ALL WOOL OVERWEAR and no underwear
Cabana   sets and gold ashtrays filled with Kip-jector Blades
by Shick
    And Ben Sira dreamed   the vision of proud patriarchs
          and medieval saints
in REMSEN SHOP FOR THE YOUNG EXECUTIVE
AND THE COLLEGE MAN trying on cuffed pants in
fitting rooms

     And Ben Sira dreamed   of the Great
     Department   Store of the Pet
shop where children on infinite afternoons flippertygib with
gerbils and goldfish and mynah birds wearing the Ecology
Shirt while Montavani plays

Jingle bells   of apples and bells and pomegranates and
mermaids and nymphs and fauns dancing around AMAZE SLEEP
SETS Precious Little by Maidenform Mix-N-Match Twin Pants
and Sweaters TIMEX ELECTRIC WATCHES *Time/Time* for
Permanent Press Pillows Pushbutton Blenders Solid State
Control Pollimex-Mist-N-Curl Soda
King Water
ford
Crystal
Gripidee
Pull-a-Tune
Pony
Gimpy's
Pal Pokey

APOLLO-Z ZEM XXI ZEROID EXPLORER MODULE

And

Ben

Sira

The Second Vision: Ben Sira in the Mystic Bookshop

DO NOT LEAVE YOUR
BICYCLE OUTSIDE, BRING
IT IN

Ah   the true Mystique
in a Secret Sanskrit

                    Code   and Ben Sira dreamed
of a Mystic Bookshop   where Lapsand the Hermit
    squats on matchlike legs under   dull, naked bulbs

and testaments My Contact With Flying Saucers   And
        Ben Sira
                dreamed   of a Mystic
                        Bookshop where Hordes
of Hassids shake their frosty earlocks
                        stamping the snow from their boots
        leaving puddles
        browsing
                through grey threadbare books, of sitting
with hippies and Irish cops
                        round a potbellied stove
                        rapping on
Meister Eckhart and Jacob Boehme
A Manual
            O Manuel   of Sex Magic
                            The Christ and
                            Psychotherapy
                Sacred
Mushroom and the Cross

            *Armor of Light: a Technique
            of Healing the Self and Others
            Revealed Through and Presented by
            Olive C.B. Priestly*
                            Book

        Shop   where   Black
Muslims
        conduct Awareness Sessions
        with Avator Mehir Babba, juking and
ad
            justing

74

Spiritual Planes

and the day   the day grows dark unnoticed

and we are all of us

with the Pistis Sophia o
Holy

Motherof
Her   Presence
/
In

dwelling

Her   Her

Astral

Her

Menses

The Third Vision: Ben Sira in the Plaza Hotel

And Ben Sira dreamed of a Plaza Hotel
where the lights of chandeliers
glisten on the wings
of angels
And Ben Sira dreamed
of a Plaza Hotel
where cherubim work the switchboards
and washroom attendants refuse tips
and pay toilets are prohibited
and the callgirls give it free

                   Plaza Hotel where Hare Krishnites assignate
with Playboy Bunnies
                  and the Chinese Communist delegation to the UN
                  has evening cocktails with
                            Daughters of the American Revolution
          and the Christian Fellowship chants
                        kama sutras in the coffeeshop performing

          all manner of unnatural

acts, while West Indian ladies
                        in pants suits
                                tip the bellhops with a blowjob

      where the luxuriant couches are empty
                          because the people are on their feet
              dancing on the carpets
           moving their limbs in ecstasy
                            and the gold spittoons
          are spitless and cigarless
                        and the telephone booths are abandoned

      where the convention rooms are filled
                          with berbers reading Dead Sea Scrolls
and the Texas oil millionaire   in the rooftop suite
      pays a grand a night for a flat-chested Salvation Army girl
                                and both are satisfied
                      and the posh Golden Ballroom
        is filled with Indians and Eskimos and ghettoblacks
             doing horas with topless WASP receptionists
      and management what's more loves it
                        and everyone knows

there are rooms in the Plaza Hotel
                where no one has ever been
                where no one will ever go
        rooms of light and darkness

                        with closets that will never be opened
                                        containing
                        eternally naked

                        Coathangers

Acknowledgements

Many texts were utilized in the preparation of this poem, and passages from a number of these have found their way into the work itself. Most frequently quoted, of course, are the Old and New Testaments and the First and Second Book of Maccabees (considered apochryphal by Jews and Protestants, but canonized by Catholics). In addition, direct or indirect quotes have been taken from the following texts: *The Christian Year*, Epistles and Gospels translated by J.B. Philips, The Macmillan Company, 1961; *Encyclopedia Brittanica*, William Benton, 1958; *Reason and Existenz*, Karl Jaspers, translated by William Earle, The Noonday Press, 1955; *Existence and Being*, Martin Heidegger, translated by Werner Bock, Henry Regnery Company, 1949; *Pistis Sophia*, translated by G.R.S. Mead, John M. Watkins, (London), 1963; *Fragments of a Faith Forgotten*, translated by G.R.S. Mead, University Books, Inc., 1960; the *I Ching*, translated by James Legge, Dover Publications, Inc. 1963; *Modern Man In Search Of A Soul*, C.G. Jung, translated by W.S. Dell and Cary F. Baynes, Harcourt, Brace and World, 1933; *The Egyptian Book of the Dead*, translated by E.A. Wallis Budge, Dover Publications Inc., 1967; Introduction to *Matthew*, Anchor Bible, W.E. Albright and C.S. Mann, Doubleday and Company, 1971; *Sabbath and Holiday Prayer Book*, translation from the Hebrew based on Rev. S. Singer's Daily Prayer Book, Hebrew Publishing Company, 1925; *The Enchiridion on Faith, Hope and Love*, St. Augustine, translated by J.F. Shaw, Henry Regnery Company, 1961; *Are You Running With Me, Jesus?*, Malcolm Boyd, *Larousse World Mythology*, edited by Pierre Grimal, Prometheus Press, 1965.